10 Publishing
a division of 10 of those.com

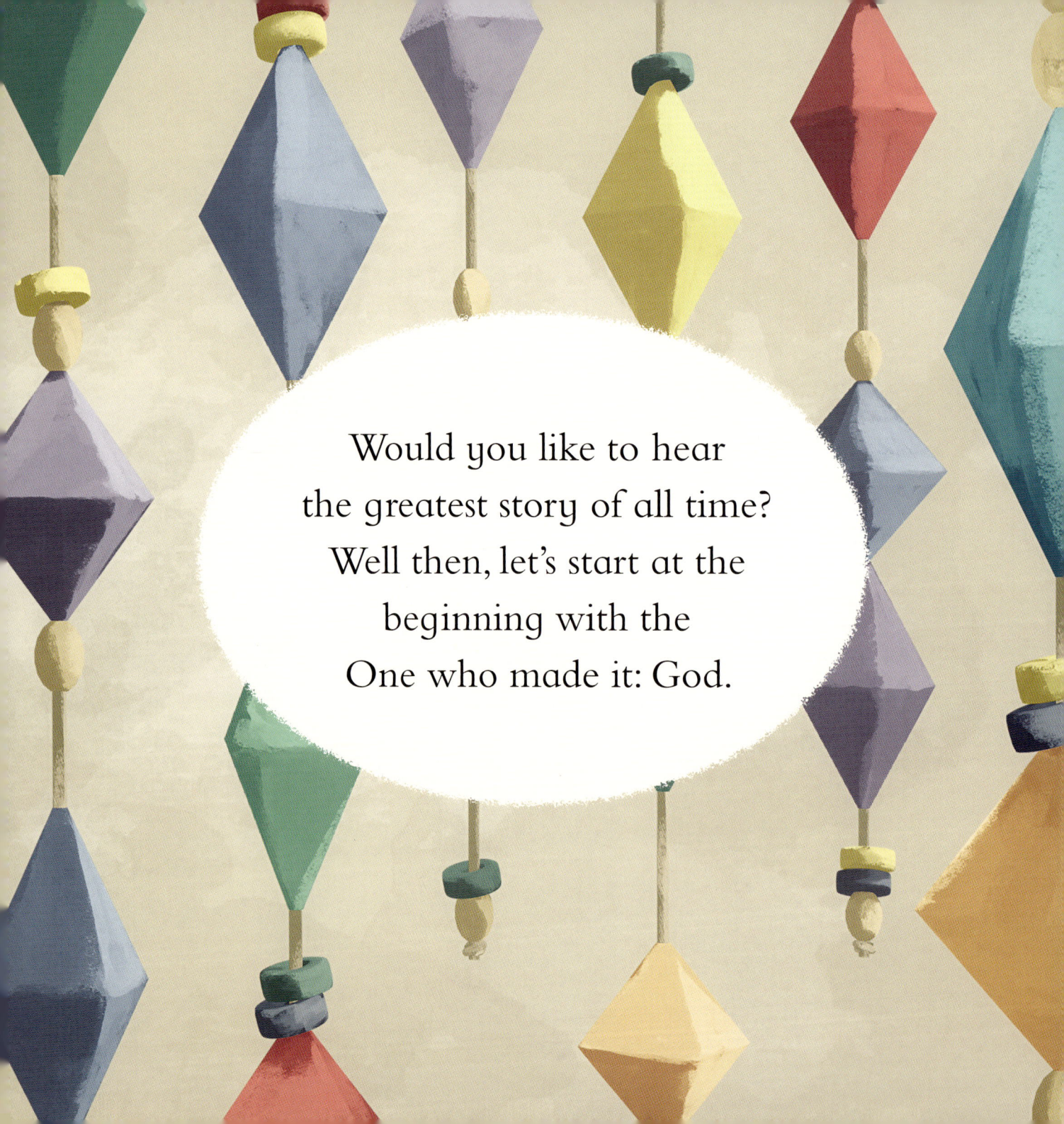

Would you like to hear
the greatest story of all time?
Well then, let's start at the
beginning with the
One who made it: God.

Everything that is all around us
was created by God.

He released the clouds from his hand and hung the stars in the sky. He dressed the trees with leaves and taught brooks to babble.

God even made the first people and
breathed on them to wake them up to life.

Their names were Adam and Eve.
They loved each other
and the world around them,
and most of all, they loved God.

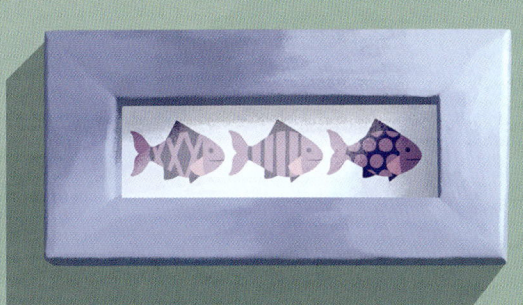

Everything was perfect.

But things aren't perfect
and wonderful today.
All of us have moments of
sickness, fear, and sadness.

What happened?

Well, God had put Adam and Eve in charge of the world and everything in it… with just one rule:

Don't eat fruit from
a certain tree.

But God had an enemy; his name was Satan.
He didn't like God or God's perfect world.
He wanted to mess it up.

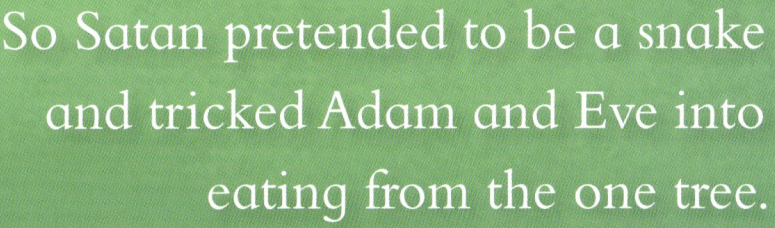

So Satan pretended to be a snake
and tricked Adam and Eve into
eating from the one tree.

Tasting the fruit sounded like a good idea, so Adam and Eve disobeyed God's one rule.

With that one bite, Adam and Eve lost their perfect friendship with God.

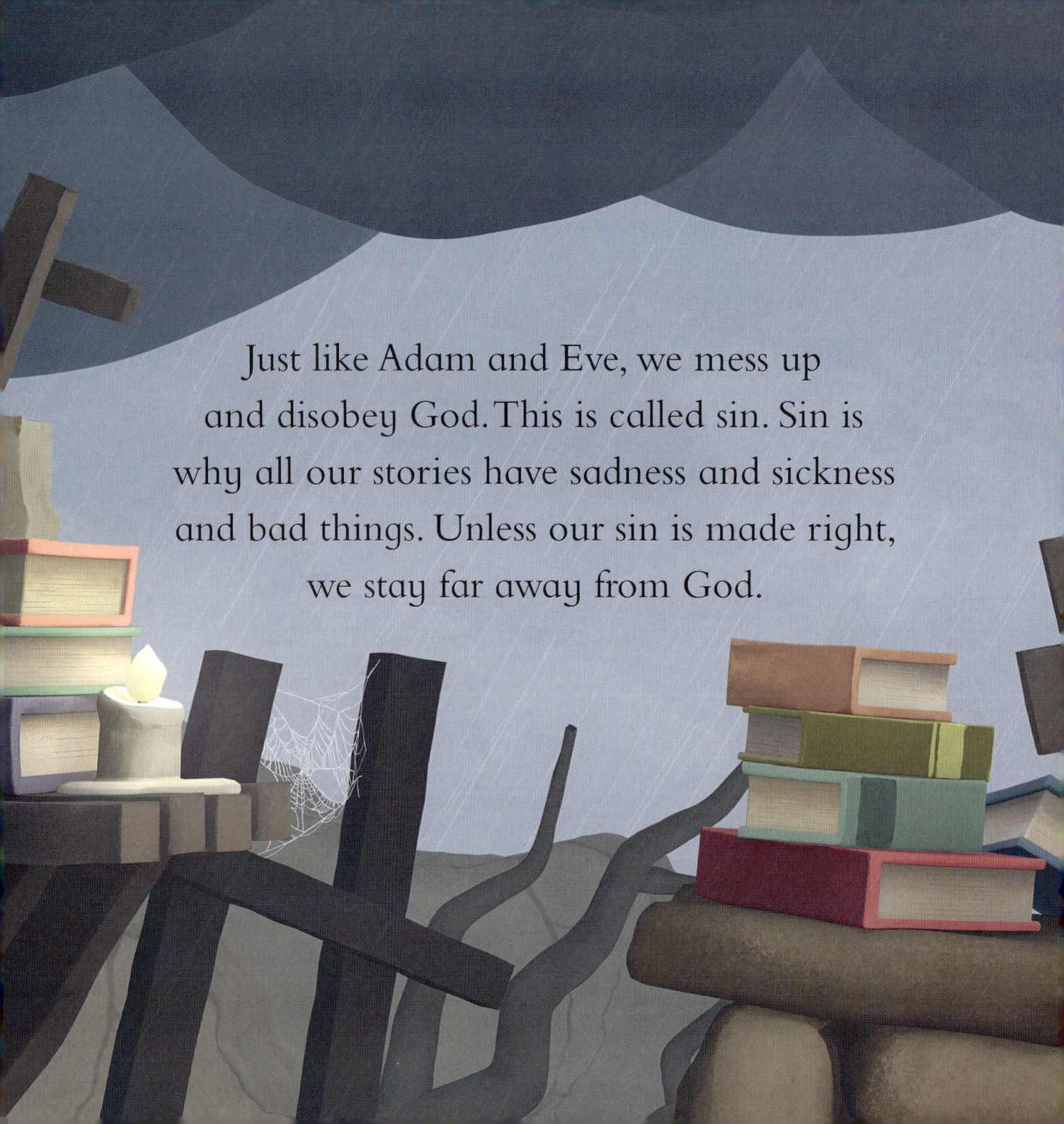

Just like Adam and Eve, we mess up
and disobey God. This is called sin. Sin is
why all our stories have sadness and sickness
and bad things. Unless our sin is made right,
we stay far away from God.

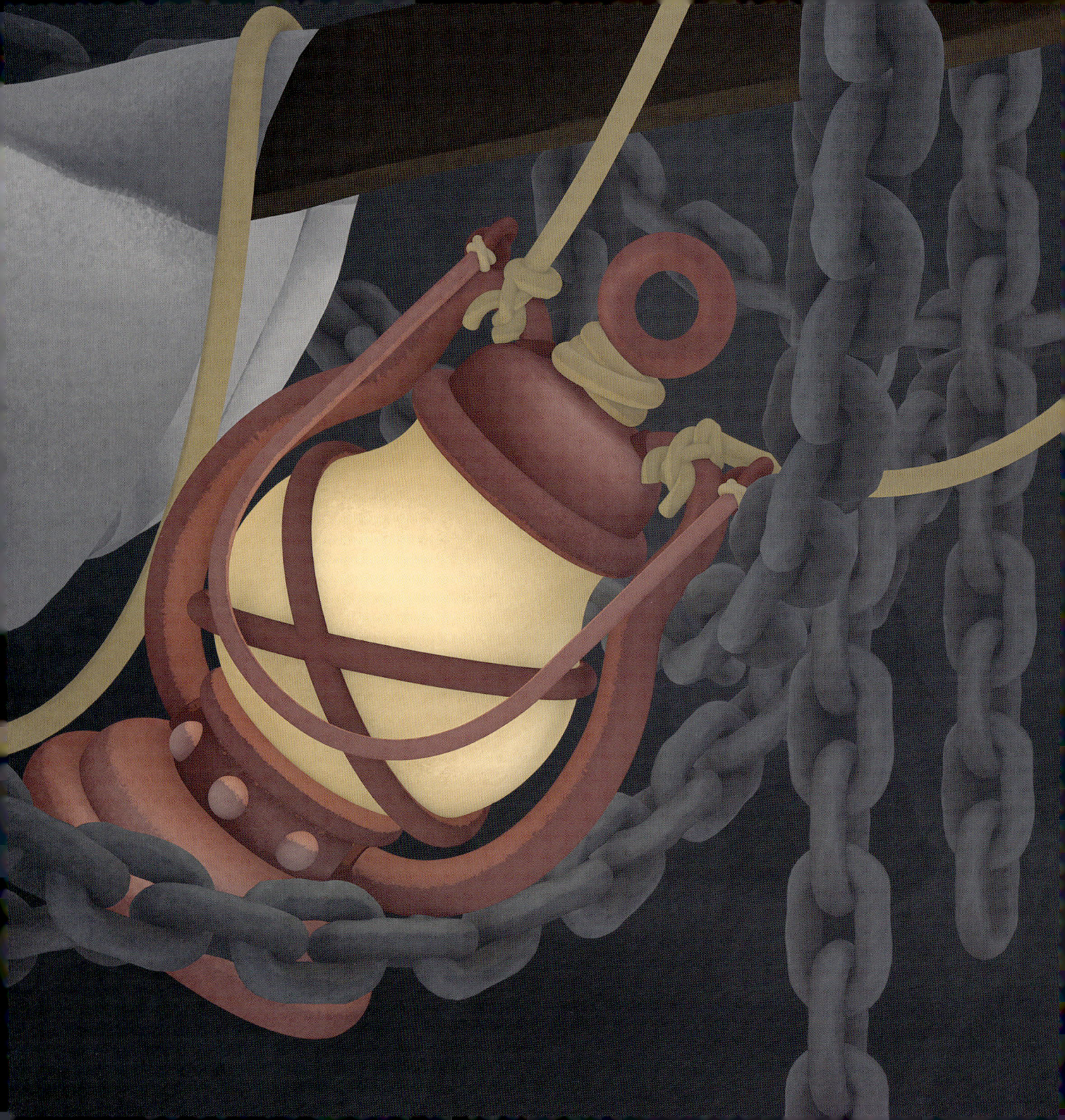

Our sin is a big deal,
but God's love is bigger.
Right after Adam and Eve
sinned, God promised that
one day someone would
come to rescue us from sin.

Who would
it be?

Well, it was God himself!
God made himself a baby,
born to a young woman named Mary.
She named him Jesus.

Just like us, Jesus grew up
and lived out all kinds of stories.
But unlike us, Jesus never sinned
and always loved Father God.

When Jesus was a grownup,
he started teaching about God's story
and did amazing things called miracles
to prove he was God.

Some people didn't like
Jesus though. They lied to
get him in trouble and
had him killed on a cross.

Jesus could have stopped
them, but he didn't.
Because he loved us so much,
he chose to die for our sins.

Everyone who loved Jesus
was so sad that he died.
They cried as they buried him.

But three days later,
Jesus came back to life!
He came back to prove
his love was bigger than sin.

Today, Jesus is sitting in heaven
and is King over everything.

This is the true story of how Jesus came to
rescue us from sin, just as God promised.

So what's next in God's story?

God made another
promise that one day,
everything in the world
will be perfect again.

He will make us a new home
with no more sin.
Everything that causes us pain
and sadness will be gone.

God also promises to be friends with us forever.

The moment you trust in Jesus'
story of rescue, God comes
near and won't ever leave.

Being forever friends with
God starts today and goes
on and on and on, because
God's story never ends.

Would you like to be a
part of God's forever story?

Well, God made a way
through Jesus, and even
though we choose to sin,
God still loves us very much.
If you are sorry for your sins
and believe Jesus is your
only rescue, God will forgive
you and make you a part
of his story forever.

The Story Maker Text © 2025 Spread Truth. Illustrations © 2025 Spread Truth.
Written by Jerry McCorkle and Erin Straza.

First published by Spread Truth in 2018.

ISBN: 978-1-83728-0-414

Published by 10Publishing, a division of 10ofThose Ltd., Tomlinson Road, Leyland, Lancs, PR25 2DY, England.
info@10ofthose.com | www.10ofthose.com

Illustrated by Phil Borst
Designed by Diane Warnes

1 3 5 7 10 9 8 6 4 2

Printed in India

This book is produced in partnership with Spread Truth.
To find out more and watch **The Story Maker** video visit: **thestorymaker.com**

10Publishing is committed to publishing quality Christian
resources that are biblical, accessible and point people to Jesus.

www.10ofthose.com is our online retail partner selling
thousands of quality books at discounted prices.

For information contact: **info@10ofthose.com**
or check out our website: **www.10ofthose.com**